CARMELLA HARRIS-BROWN

This book is a work of non-fiction. Unless otherwise noted, the author and the publisher make
no explicit guarantees as to the accuracy of the information contained in this book and in
some cases, names of people and places have been altered to protect their privacy.

WestBow Press books may be ordered through booksellers or by contacting:

WestBow Press
A Division of Thomas Nelson & Zondervan
1663 Liberty Drive
Bloomington, IN 47403
www.westbowpress.com
844-714-3454

ISBN: 978-1-6642-1115-5 (sc)
ISBN: 978-1-6642-1116-2 (e)

Library of Congress Control Number: 2020921672

Print information available on the last page.

WestBow Press rev. date: 02/15/2021

WESTBOW
PRESS®
A DIVISION OF THOMAS NELSON
& ZONDERVAN

Hey!
I See You!

¡Oye!
¡Te veo!

CONTENTS

DEDICATION

This book is dedicated to the memory of my loving parents George and Anna.

Hey, I see you breaking through the ground with lovely petals all around. I always see you in the summertime. They call you a flower.

Oye, te veo rompiendo, a trav'es de la el suelo con hermosos pe'talos a tu alrededor. Siempre te veo en verano. Te llaman flor.

Hey, I see you on ground so prickly and green all around. You're everywhere I can see. Your colors change in the fall. They call you grass.

Oye, te veo en el suelo tan espinoso y verde por todos lados. Estas en todos los lugares que puedo ver. Tus colores cambian en el otono. Te llaman cesped.

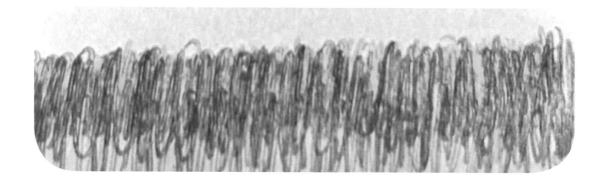

Hey, I see you down under my feet. You are dark and dusty to me. You help to grow food, plants, flowers and grass. They use you to build houses too. They call you dirt.

Oye, Te veo mis pies. Me ves oscura y polvorienta para mi. Ayudas a cultivar alimentos plantas, flores y cesped. Tambi'en te usan para construir casas. Te llaman mugre.

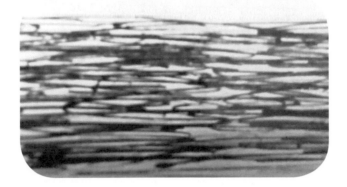

Hey, I see you standing so tall waving your branches all around. Your leaves can be green, brown, and multicolored too. Your trunk is strong big and brown. They call you a tree.

Oye, te veo de pie muy alto y agitando tus ramas alrededor. Tus hojas pueden ser de color verde, marron y multicolores. Tu tronco es fuerte, grande y marron. Te llaman arbol.

Hey, I see you up there in the sky moving all around. You're sometimes gray, blue or white you have many shapes. They call you clouds.

Oye, te veo alla' arriba en el cielo moviendote por todas partes. Tu eres a veces gris, azul, o blanco tienes muchas formas. Te llaman nubes.

Hey, I see you dropping down from the sky and you're wet like the water in my tub. You help to grow fruits, vegetables flowers, grass and trees. They call you rain.

Oye, te veo caer del cielo y estas mojado como el agua de mi banera. Ayudas a cultivar frutas, verduras, flores, cesped y arboles. Te llaman lluvia.

Hey, I see you a flashing light with a roaring sound like a lion. You can be very loud, but I'm not afraid. They call you thunder and lighting.

Oye, te veo una luz intermitente con un sonido rugiente como un leon. Puedes ser muy ruidoso pero no tengo miedo. Te llaman truenos y relampagos.

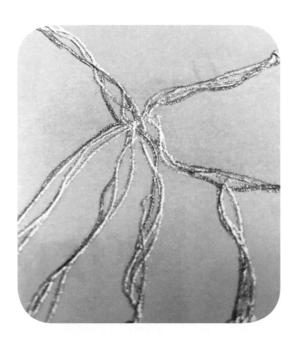

Hey, I see you high in the sky sometimes hidden by the clouds. Your light is very bright and you warm the earth too. They call you the sun.

Oye, te veo en lo alto del cielo, a veces estas oculto por las nubes. Tu luz es on tan brillante. Tambien calientas la tierra. Te llaman el sol.

Hey, I see you up there in the sky with those amazing colors to my eyes. I see you after the rain. They call you a rainbow.

Oye, te veo alla' arriba en el cielo con esos colores hermosos que asombran mis ojos. Te veo despues de la lluvia. Te llaman arcoiris.

Hey, I see you on the ground wiggling all around. You come out after the rain. I've seen you in many colors and sizes too. They call you a worm.

Oye, te veo en el tierra menearse moveiendote por todos lados. Sales venir despues de la lluvia. Tambi'en te he visto de muchos colores y tamanos. Te llaman gusano.

Hey, I see you so very strong going in and out of that big hill. You carry large and small things across the ground as you work fast preparing for the winter. They call you an ant.

Oye, te veo tan mismo fuerte entrando y saliendo de esa gran colina. Tu lleva cosas grandes y pequenas por el tierra mientras trabaja ra'pido preparandote para el invierno. Te llaman hormiga.

Hey, I see you moving slowly on the ground. You flew to a flower and then to a leaf. You have beautiful colors on your wings. I tried to touch you, but you flew away. They call you a ladybug.

Oye, te veo moviendote lentamente en el tierra. Vuelas a una flor y luego a una hoja. Tienes colores hermosos en tus alas. Trate' de tocarte, pero tehuir. Te llaman mariquita.

Hey, I see you flying over my head, but sometimes you sit on a fence, bench or a branch. You make funny sounds that is called squawking . They call you a bird.

Oye, te veo volando sobre mi cabeza pero a veces te sientas en el banco de la cerca o en una rama. Haces sonidos graciosos que se llaman gaznidos. Te llaman pa'jaro.

Hey, What's your name? _____

Oye, cual es tu nombre? _____

You can find the release of my upcoming books

I Like Who I Am
Guess Who I Am
Let's Have Fun
What's your favorite season?
The Magical Book
It's not your fault

On my Instagram @lots2learn1234

ABOUT THE AUTHOR

Carmella Harris-Brown is a wife and mother of four beautiful creative children Kendall, Keyshawn, Kaleb and Kirsten. She enjoys reading and loves children. One of her greatest joys is to see the light that appears in the eyes of a child as they discover something new. What inspired her to write this book are the memories of her children first experiences with nature, animals and insects. Carmella wanted to give to her children a book to share with their families and friends. She hopes that you enjoy this book as much as she enjoyed writing it.

Printed in the United States
By Bookmasters